BLACK HOLES

EXPLAINED

THE MYSTERIES OF SPACE

BLACK HOLES
EXPLAINED

JAMES NEGUS

Enslow Publishing
101 W. 23rd Street
Suite 240
New York, NY 10011
USA
enslow.com

Published in 2019 by Enslow Publishing, LLC.
101 W. 23rd Street, Suite 240, New York, NY 10011

Copyright © 2019 by Enslow Publishing, LLC.
All rights reserved.

No part of this book may be reproduced by any means without the written permission of the publisher.

Library of Congress Cataloging-in-Publication Data

Names: Negus, James, author.
Title: Black holes explained / James Negus.
Description: New York : Enslow Publishing, [2019] | Series: The mysteries of space | Audience: Grades 7-12. | Includes bibliographical references and index.
Identifiers: LCCN 2017052667| ISBN 9780766099623 (library bound) | ISBN 9780766099630 (pbk.)
Subjects: LCSH: Black holes (Astronomy)—Juvenile literature. | Cosmology—Juvenile literature.
Classification: LCC QB843.B55 N44 2018 | DDC 523.8/875—dc23
LC record available at https://lccn.loc.gov/2017052667

Printed in the United States of America

To Our Readers: We have done our best to make sure all website addresses in this book were active and appropriate when we went to press. However, the author and the publisher have no control over and assume no liability for the material available on those websites or on any websites they may link to. Any comments or suggestions can be sent by email to customerservice@enslow.com.

Photos Credits: Cover RedPixel.pl/ Shutterstock.com; p. 5 d1sk/Shutterstock.com; p. 7 NASA/Science Photo Library/Getty Images; pp. 8, 21 Mark Garlick /Science Source; p. 11 Archive Photos/Getty Images; p. 14 NASA/CXC/SAO; p. 15 Stocktrek Images/Getty Images; p. 16 Barcroft Media/Getty Images; p. 19 Larry Landolfi/Science Source/Getty Images; p. 22 Designua/Shutterstock.com; p. 25 Print Collector/Hulton Archive/Getty Images; p. 28 Bloomberg/Getty Images; p. 33 NASA; p. 35 Crystal Eye Studio/Shutterstock.com; p. 36 peresanz /Shutterstock.com; p. 40 Ron Miller/Stocktrek Images/Getty Images; p. 43 Benjamin Bromley/Science Source; p. 45 AFP/Getty Images; p. 47 Yurkoman/Shutterstock.com; pp. 49, 51 Mark Garlick/Science Photo Library/Getty Images; p. 55 Fouad A. Saad/Shutterstock.com; p. 57 NASA/ESA/STSCI/W. Colley & E. Turner, Princeton/ Science Photo Library/Getty Images; p. 60 Lionel Flusin/Gamma-Rapho /Getty Images; p. 62 Richard Kail/Science Photo Library/Getty Images; p. 63 Bruno Vincent/Getty Images; back cover and interior pages sdecoret/Shutterstock.com (earth's atmosphere from space), clearviewstock/Shutterstock.com (space and stars).

CONTENTS

Introduction
6

Chapter One
The Birth of a Giant
10

Chapter Two
A Galactic Heart
18

Chapter Three
Cosmic Exploration
24

Chapter Four
Merging Companions
31

Chapter Five
The Event Horizon
38

Chapter Six
A Cosmic Worm
46

Chapter Seven
Miniature Black Holes
53

Chapter Eight
A Black Hole's Fate
61

Chapter Notes 68
Glossary 75
Further Reading 77
Index 79

INTRODUCTION

"My god—this may be it!" renowned theoretical physicist Kip Thorne exclaimed.[1] The former colleague of the beloved astronomer Carl Sagan had just inspected data confirming a monumental milestone in astrophysic—the detection of gravitational waves, predicted to exist by Albert Einstein in 1916.[2] The observations were detected by the Earth-based Laser Interferometer Gravitational-Wave Observatory (LIGO) on December 26, 2015.[3,4] For the first time, the merger of two black holes was measured.

For many, though, the sources detected by LIGO—black holes—are somewhat of a mystery. Far from the radiant gemlike images of stars, the deep colorful hues of planetary atmospheres, or majestic nebulas appearing as cosmic flowers, black holes are often depicted as dark, holelike regions in the very fabric of space.

However, the true nature of black holes reveals them as one of the universe's most astounding creations. What they lack in visual beauty, they compensate for in shear power and size. In fact, these immense cosmic formations are pockets of space estimated to be up to several billion times the mass of our sun; the largest ever being seventeen billion times the mass of

INTRODUCTION

This is a conceptual model of a black hole. Matter rotates around the center of the black hole due to the strong gravitational forces. Matter can also fall directly into the center of the spherical core.

the sun.[5] As a result, this concentration of mass forms a very strong gravitational pull on matter nearby.

Consider the sun; it contains 99 percent of the mass in the solar system. Consequently, it gravitationally influences matter in this region, such as planets, asteroids, and comets, to orbit around it. If the sun is responsible for the orbit and pull of all the planets and matter in the solar system, envision the gravitational influence of a black hole, billions of times more massive, on matter in its vicinity.

Given the scale of black holes, one would not be wrong to assume they are rare. However, astronomers currently estimate that there may be a black hole at the center of every galaxy,

The supermassive black hole Sagittarius A* resides at the center of the Milky Way galaxy. Multiple stars orbit around the core of the black hole.

including Earth's home galaxy, the Milky Way. As a result of the Milky Way's proximity, scientists on Earth can use the local black hole, Sagittarius A*, as a source of study.

Moreover, research indicates that most black holes in fact form from stars.[6] While our sun is a star, it will not make the transformation, however. This is due to the mass requirement of three solar masses for a star to become a stellar black hole, where one solar mass represents the mass of our sun.

Astronomers theorize that one out of every one thousand stars has enough mass to create a stellar black hole. Considering an average galaxy contains at least one hundred billion stars, this equates to at least one hundred million stellar mass black holes able to be formed per galaxy![7]

Furthermore, throughout history, different forms of instrumentation and technology have been utilized to physically detect and study these cosmic spectacles. These missions have led the way for future endeavors, such as the National Aeronautics and Space Administration's (NASA) Imaging X-Ray Polarimetry Explorer (IXPE), anticipated to launch in 2020.[8] This mission will explore the intense gravitational fields and gases near the core of black holes, which may help answer the daunting question "What happens when matter travels into the center of a black hole?"

Chapter One

The Birth of a Giant

Astronomy is the study of celestial objects and phenomena; it is the oldest of all natural sciences in human history. Since ancient times, civilizations have continually sought an understanding of their place in the universe. Unlike many of the physical sciences, only the naked eye is required to practice observational astronomy.

Among the wide range of cosmic objects that have long been analyzed by humans, from planets to galaxies to asteroids, stars have long remained a primary source of observation. Ancient Indian, Greek, Babylonian, Chinese, Egyptian, and Mayan civilizations meticulously logged stellar catalogues and positions, and they relied upon the stars for navigation.

Stars continue to remain major sources of observation in modern-day astronomy. This persistent exploration of stars can be attributed to their prevalence in the night sky. In fact, astronomers estimate at least one hundred billion stars reside

THE BIRTH OF A GIANT

> The Greek astronomer Hipparchus (c. 190 BCE–120 BCE) is credited with accurately modeling the motion of the sun and moon, as well as creating the first comprehensive star catalog.

within every galaxy, such as the Milky Way, and that at least two hundred billion galaxies exist within the universe.[1] Earth receives light from many of these stellar sources that are scattered throughout the cosmos.

Stellar Life

As civilizations evolved so too did the tools used to analyze stars. Shortly after the turn of the twentieth century, astronomers discovered that stars are actually massive, incredibly hot furnaces that produce vast amounts of energy. This energy is primarily produced through the fusion (combining) of hydrogen atoms into a heavier byproduct, helium. As this process unfolds, excess energy is generated in the form of light that radiates, or emits, away from the star. This is the light seen when gazing at the stars above. However, as the fusion of elements within

11

stars continually occurs, over millions or billions of years, a limit to further combinations is met. For stars at least three times the mass of the sun, this signifies the impending birth of what astronomers term a black hole.

ANCIENT ASTRONOMY

Ancient astronomers considered celestial objects to be linked with the gods, spirits, and passage of time. They also associated cosmic events with signs of impending natural events, such as rain, drought seasons, and tides.

The origins of Western astronomy are tied to Mesopotamia, where the ancient kingdom of Babylonia was located. The earliest Babylonian star catalog dates back to 1200 BCE.

Astronomy in India and China was used to track the passage of time and create calendars in the third millennium BCE and the sixth century BCE.

Comparatively, the ancient Greeks developed three-dimensional models to explain the apparent motion of the planets around the fourth century BCE.

The Egyptians also relied upon astronomy around the third millennium BCE to precisely align the Egyptian pyramids with the pole star.

Cosmic Transformation

At the end of the seventeenth century, astronomer, physicist, and mathematician Isaac Newton (1642–1727) published his theory of gravity. Newton's theory indicates that particles attract to one another with a force that is related to their mass and distance.[2] Newton was able to show that less massive objects in the universe are attracted to more massive objects. The force described here is the gravitational force and exists throughout the universe. In stars with enough mass, this force is responsible for the transition to a black hole.

Specifically, as massive stars continue to fuse elements in their cores, their masses increase, and so does their gravitational pull. The gravitational force that attracts more matter to the core of the star is balanced by excess energy released from elements fusing in the star's core. This interaction between gravitational force and outward energy is what enables a star to remain stable. However, once the elements can no longer combine, there is no outward force to balance the inward pull of gravity. At this stage, the star's central core begins to collapse, heats up, and becomes extremely dense. The star then contracts and matter bounces off the core, ejecting much of the contents of the star into space. This process is known as a supernova. Once much of the star's outer layers are expelled into space, what remains is an extremely compact object, an infant black hole.

Stellar Black Hole Emergence

From the cataclysmic death of a star at least three times the mass of the sun, a region of space not visible in any wavelength is birthed. As the star's outer shell is expelled into space, creating an

BLACK HOLES EXPLAINED

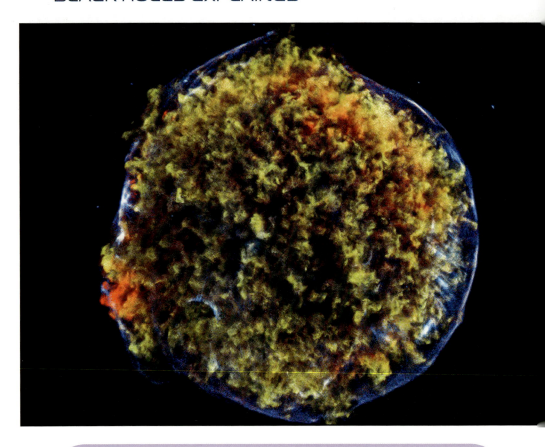

This Tycho Supernova Remnant image shows stellar layers being expelled into space from a supernova explosion. At the center of this explosion is an extremely dense stellar core.

explosion that can outshine its entire galaxy, an extremely dense core that is left collapses onto itself and transforms into what astronomers call a stellar black hole. This black hole contains a very large amount of mass in a very small volume, which produces a strong gravitational field. The gravitational field is so strong that not even light can escape certain regions. If observed through a telescope, one would not be able to observe it directly. Rather, it could only be observed by its effect on nearby matter.

THE BIRTH OF A GIANT

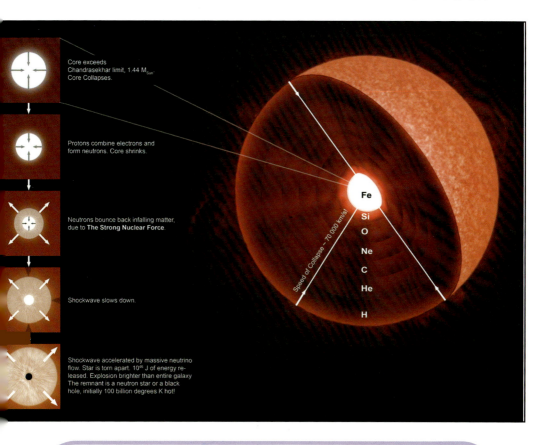

> Deep within the interior of the star, gravitational forces cause matter to compress. The extremely dense and hot core collapses, the star explodes, and only a black hole is left.

Black Hole Siblings

Though a stellar black hole has an astounding density and gravitational pull on matter nearby, astronomers have theorized that this type of black hole is at the bottom of its class.[3] In actuality, intermediate-mass black holes and supermassive black holes are the older and much larger siblings. These classes of black holes are several factors more massive than stellar black holes.

15

BLACK HOLES EXPLAINED

While stellar black holes contain the mass of three to ten times the mass of the sun, intermediate-mass black holes contain one hundred to one million solar masses. Though intermediate-mass black holes are far less understood compared to stellar black holes, astronomers have attempted to pose theories regarding their formation. In particular, research suggests that the mass of these regions is too large to have been created with the collapse of a single star.[4] Rather, their formation may have occurred

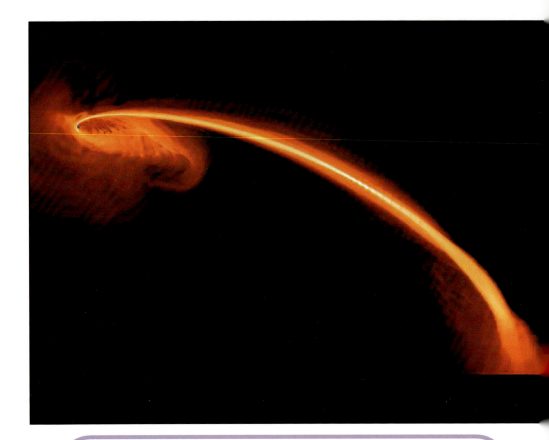

This image reveals the effects gravity can have on matter in the universe. Gas from a star is shredded as it gets sucked into a black hole. Some of the gas is also ejected into space.

through the merger of smaller stellar black holes, or the collision of many massive stars in tightly packed stellar clusters.

Intermediate-mass black holes are impressive, however, the big brother in the family is unquestionably the supermassive black hole. These giants dwarf stellar black holes and severely outrank intermediate-mass black holes. Estimates place the mass of these cosmic regions at hundreds of thousands to billions of solar masses.[5]

Though, similar to intermediate-mass black holes, not much is understood about how supermassive black holes form. Astronomers propose their existence could stem from the merger of lower mass black holes. Another possibility is that as stellar black holes and intermediate-mass black holes formed, they gravitationally attracted more matter over a long enough time and created a chain reaction of matter flowing in, which attracted more matter. Matter falling into the black hole would then cause a steady accumulation of additional particles onto the black hole.

So what kind of effects can black holes have on their environment? Experts theorize that every galaxy contains a supermassive black hole at its core. Given the astounding mass of a supermassive black hole, how does its central galactic location impact nearby matter? What about black hole influence on galactic structure?

Chapter Two

A Galactic Heart

Earth is a small planetary body in the universe; it exists within the Milky Way, home to more than one hundred billion stars. Galaxies, such as the Milky Way, harbor an astounding collection of cosmic objects, which include stars, gas, dust, planets, asteroids, comets, dark matter, and even concentrated stellar populations such as nebulas and globular clusters. On a clear night in North America, one can look toward the southern horizon and in the constellation Sagittarius notice a distinct hazy band that traverses the night sky. For many, this band is initially believed to be clouds or light pollution; however, this is in fact the center of the Milky Way galaxy! Though it may be difficult to perceive with the human eye, the densest region of the haze is what is termed the "galactic bulge," the center of our galaxy.[1] Within this region is a vast collection of stars, dust, and gas, and at the heart of this matter is the opaque monstrous supermassive black hole Sagittarius A*.

Gravitational Well

Black holes have gravitational pulls so strong that not even light can escape their cores. Thus, astronomers had to rely upon other means to verify the existence of a black hole at the center of the Milky Way. For Sagittarius A*, scientists realized that by studying the gas and dust near the galactic center, they would be able to confirm the existence of Sagittarius A*.

Particularly, gas and dust near the center of a black hole are strongly drawn in by the black hole's immense gravitational influence. Once close enough, their velocities become greater as they orbit closer and closer. As a result of the fast motion of particles falling into the black hole, temperatures can reach several millions of degrees. These temperatures create other forms of energy near the black hole that are able to be studied.

This hazy band lining the sky is the center of the Milky Way. In the middle of the band is a bright center, where the Milky Way's supermassive black hole resides.

Specifically, as matter is heated, it can emit light at different energies, some of which can be observed, while others cannot. In the case of Sagittarius A*, radio, infrared, and X-ray energy are types of energy that astronomers can see even though visual observations are blocked out. These energies were used to observe the extremely hot matter falling into the center of our galaxy and confirm that a supermassive black hole exists there.

Common Center

Of the two hundred billion galaxies believed to occupy the observable universe, there are three primary types of galaxies: elliptical, spiral, and lenticular. Elliptical galaxies are smooth and featureless galaxies that are in the shape of an ellipse, appearing as a circle that has been stretched from its center. Spiral galaxies, such as the Milky Way, have a flattened disk with a band of stars forming a spiral structure; these galaxies can also form a bar of stars that extend from their cores. Finally, lenticular galaxies have a bright central bulge and are surrounded by a disk-like structure but do not contain spirals.[2] Among these galaxy types, a central black hole is believed to exist at the center of each. Astronomers have two prevailing theories for how black holes wound up in the centers of these galaxies. They propose that either matter in a certain region of space was relatively concentrated and eventually gave rise to a black hole, which over time pulled in more matter as a source of growth, or a black hole formed first and continued to grow by absorbing gas, dust, and other cosmic matter around it.[3] Research seeks to determine this, though it is clear that once black holes form, they continue to attract local and interstellar (space between the stars) dust and matter to grow the galaxies they inhabit.

A GALACTIC HEART

Lenticular (*top left*), spiral (*bottom left*), irregular (*top right*), and elliptical (*bottom right*) galaxies are shown.

Intergalactic Light

In the early twentieth century, Albert Einstein published his theory of general relativity and successfully predicted the concept of gravitational lensing.[4, 5] He conveyed the idea that matter and energy travel throughout space and time relative to the physical geometry of space. A good way to envision the basic principle of his theory is to imagine placing a bowling ball on a large trampoline. The mass of the bowling ball will cause the center of the trampoline to sink toward the ground. Now imagine trying to roll a golf ball or pour water on the trampoline. The path of the ball or water will be dramatically affected by the curvature of the trampoline. The ball and the flow of water will be directed

BLACK HOLES EXPLAINED

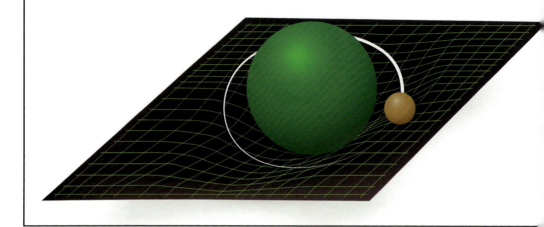

GENERAL RELATIVITY (gravity)

The principle of general relativity can be represented with two balls and a soft surface. Massive objects within the universe create depressions in the fabric of space that cause smaller objects to rotate around them.

toward the center of the trampoline, in the location that the bowling ball rests. Similarly, as matter or energy approaches a very dense region in space, their paths are altered toward it.

Light Path

On the scale of the universe, when light from a source is emitted, it can be observed from Earth. Consider what happens when a galaxy that contains a supermassive black hole, a galaxy similar to the Milky Way, is in the path of this light.

As discussed, a supermassive black hole can contain the mass of several billion solar masses. Consequently, there is

ALBERT EINSTEIN

Albert Einstein was a theoretical physicist and mathematician born in Germany on March 14, 1879. He developed the theory of relativity and is considered to be one of the most influential physicists of the twentieth century. He was awarded the Nobel Prize in Physics in 1921.

In 1916 Einstein formulated the theory of general relativity, which explains that the force of gravity arises from the curvature in space-time. This led to the prediction that a compact mass could deform space-time enough to form a black hole.

such a strong gravitational pull that even light merely passing by is not safe from the influence of a black hole. The photons (light) literally bend as they pass through black holes on their way to Earth. This event is so prominent that it can even be viewed through Earth-based telescopes such as the Keck Observatory in Mauna Kea, Hawaii.[6]

Supermassive black holes significantly influence light and matter in their vicinity and thus remain a central topic of interest in the astronomical community. In addition, the scope of black hole research is growing significantly as technology continues to improve. Considering the continued scientific attraction, what will future missions seek to uncover about these cosmic regions?

Chapter Three

Cosmic Exploration

Black holes, from stellar to supermassive, prevent visible light from escaping their gravitational fields. As a result, studying regions that cannot be viewed directly with optical telescopes has proven a challenging endeavor for astronomers. To address this difficulty, scientists are forced to rely upon alternative techniques for analysis.

Elusive Target

Considering the difficult nature of studying black holes directly, it is not surprising that the first black hole was not officially reported until 1971, though Einstein initially predicted their existence in 1916.[1] The discovery of this black hole, Cygnus X-1, was initially detected with instruments on a rocket launched from New

COSMIC EXPLORATION

Mexico in 1964. Through this observation, it was revealed that a very important method could be used by scientists to study objects that are not visible—the electromagnetic spectrum.[2]

Revealing Light

Energy throughout the universe travels in the form of energetic photons. In the year 1800, William Herschel (1738–1822) sought to further understand the nature of light in the universe. Specifically, he passed sunlight through a prism. The prism—a piece of glass that refracts, or bends, light—separated the light into a rainbow of colors. Once the light was separated into a rainbow of colors, Herschel measured the temperature under each color, including beyond where the colors ended. His experiment showed that the temperature seemingly out of the light was the highest.[3] What Herschel

William Herschel analyzes the spectrum of light. His analysis revealed that there are forms of energy not visible to the naked eye.

25

BLACK HOLES EXPLAINED

discovered was that measurements of light could be made beyond what could visually be seen!

Herschel's discovery led to the origin of the electromagnetic spectrum, which describes a range of light energies that include radio waves, microwaves, infrared, ultraviolet, X-rays, and gammas rays, in increasing order of energy. This property of light provided astronomers a particularly useful alternative method to observe black holes—energetic X-ray emissions.

Energetic Observations

To understand why X-ray emission is essential, consider that black holes funnel in gas, dust, and cosmic debris within close proximity of their strong gravitational fields. As this matter is drawn inward, it begins to rotate around the center of the black hole, where it then experiences an increase in velocity and rotational speed. Envision a drain at the base of a sink. If the sink is filled with water and the drain is opened, water will begin to flow toward the hole as it flows through. As water gets closer to the drain, its velocity and rotational speed are increased compared to water farther from the drain. Similarly, matter speeds up as it gets closer to the center of a black hole. This increase in speed leads to matter being more energetic, and thus results in gas and dust being heated to millions of degrees. As a consequence, matter then begins to emit high-energy photons known as X-rays. It is through this emission of X-rays that observations were able to validate the discovery of Cygnus X-1.

Space-Based Instruments

Since the discovery of Cygnus X-1, substantial progress has been made to improve the observational capabilities of black hole research. Specifically, NASA launched the Swift Gamma-Ray Burst Mission (SWIFT) into orbit in 2004. This instrument is dedicated to studying gamma-ray energy in the universe, which is emitted from the most energetic events in the cosmos.[4] A major milestone of this mission was its observation of the birth of a black hole in 2005. The source of this measurement was believed to be a young massive star collapsing into a black hole that released a burst of high-energy gamma rays.[5]

Furthermore, a primary instrument utilized for advancing the field of black hole astronomy is NASA's Chandra X-Ray Observatory. Chandra was launched in 1999 and orbits Earth to take measurements due to the fact that Earth's atmosphere blocks out most X-ray emission. This observatory is still in use and continues to enable scientists to probe into unique environments within the universe, such as regions near black holes, with X-ray images.[6] The defining moment for Chandra was the first detection of X-ray emission of Sagittarius A*, the supermassive black hole at the center of the Milky Way.

Gravitational Detection

While analyzing the various energies emitted near the core of black holes has proven extremely useful for astronomers, additional means to analyze black holes do exist. Most notable is the Laser Interferometer Gravitational-Wave Observatory (LIGO),

BLACK HOLES EXPLAINED

A scientist examines data in the control room of the Laser Interferometer Gravitational-Wave Observatory (LIGO) in Washington. LIGO is responsible for the first detection of gravitational waves from Earth.

a pivotal science campaign devoted to unraveling the nature of black holes, black hole mergers specifically. This observatory, operated by the California Institute of Technology and the Massachusetts Institute of Technology, measured very small-scale ripples caused by merging black holes for the first time in history in 2015.[7] This discovery has paved the way for additional gravitational wave observatories and will hopefully provide a better understanding of black hole mergers.

COSMIC EXPLORATION

LIGO

LIGO is the world's largest gravitational wave observatory. It consists of two laser detectors, one in Livingston, Louisiana, and one in Richland, Washington. Each observatory supports an L-shaped vacuum system, measuring 2.5 miles (4 kilometers) on each side.

LIGO detects gravitational waves by measuring slight shifts in light that are bounced off internal mirrors.

The observatories are 1,865 miles (3,002 km) apart, and since gravitational waves travel at the speed of light, the distance of the observatories corresponds to a difference in gravitational wave arrival times of up to ten milliseconds.

Future Science

Though much progress has been made in black hole astronomy, continual progress to uncover the nature of black holes is under way. Particularly, NASA has selected the Imaging Polarimetry Explorer (IXPE) mission to study the extreme environments around black holes. The mission is set to launch in 2020 and will focus on analyzing the gravitational, electric, and magnetic fields near black holes.

Astronomers persistently advocate for advancements in black hole research as there is much to be understood from these

BLACK HOLES EXPLAINED

cosmic entities. Ultimately, developing a deeper understanding of how these regions influence matter will offer vital insight on their dynamic effects. Specifically, as X-ray and gamma ray detectors improve, researchers will be able to peer further and further into regions previously not very well understood.

Given the dramatic influence that black holes at the center of galaxies can have on matter, even light, consider what occurs when these regions of space merge. LIGO has detected evidence of such a merger, but what else can occur when black holes combine? In addition, what effects can arise when matter continues to spiral into the core of a black hole?

Merging Companions

The average distance between galaxies is immense. On average, a galaxy is 3.3 million light-years from its neighbor and often much farther.[1] For reference, a single light-year is approximately 6 trillion miles (9.5 trillion km), the equivalent of 750 million Earth diameters. It would be reasonable to assume galaxies infrequently interact with each other, and in fact, most galaxies do exist in isolation for hundreds of millions of years. However, a few galaxies experience a different fate.

Galactic Pair

For select galaxies, a slight influence between their gravitational fields and a neighboring galaxy can occur. Though the gravitational interaction is initially slight, it can develop over hundreds of millions of years to significantly influence the movements of the galaxies. Imagine placing two bowling balls on opposing sides of a large trampoline. Analyzed individually, each dense ball causes the fabric of the trampoline to sink in its local area. However, over time the path of both balls moves toward the same central region of the trampoline. Similarly, supermassive black holes at the center of galaxies are extremely dense and when they are close enough to a companion galaxy, they drift toward each other. The stage is then set for a profound event, a galactic merger.

Dual Black Holes

Over time, as merging galaxies near, stars spill across the boundaries of their host galaxies due to the gravitational tug of opposing galaxies. Thus, the process of a galactic merger begins

GALAXY MERGER TYPES

Galaxy mergers can be classified as either binary or multiple. Binary mergers involve two interacting galaxies, whereas multiple mergers include more than two.

Additionally, minor and major mergers are used to classify galaxies. For a minor merger, one of the galaxies is significantly larger than the other and absorbs most of the gas and stars in the smaller one.

Major mergers occur if two spiral galaxies are approximately the same size. As they merge, they drive away dust and gas.

MERGING COMPANIONS

to fully unfold. During the merging process, the gravitational interaction between the galaxies escalates from modest to grand. The orbits of stars in both galaxies changes dramatically, and collisions of dust and gas can intensify as the companion galaxies intertwine. At the core of the galaxies, the central black holes are forced to drift closer and closer toward each other. Eventually, the strong influence of each black hole results in the pair orbiting each other. This process, the orbit of two black holes around each other, is termed a binary black hole.

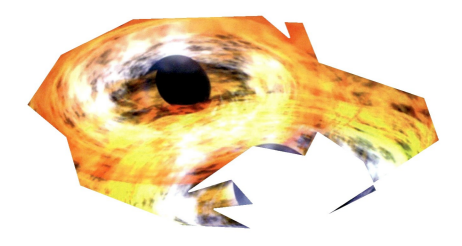

Two black holes merge into a single black hole. This process is believed to be a method in which supermassive black holes form.

Accretion Formation

As black holes orbit one another, their mutual gravitational fields disrupt stars, dust, and gas in their vicinity. Consequently, a dynamical process known as accretion can occur. This process can develop on one or both of the black holes. Accretion begins when matter near the core of a black hole is close enough to rotate directly into, rather than around, the black hole. The matter that flows onto the black hole then creates an accretion disk.

Large particles, consisting of molecules, that speed up in the accretion disk near the black hole core are broken down into individual atoms. These atoms continue to rotate, and their fast motion creates extremely hot temperatures.[2] For reference, try rubbing your palms together faster and faster; as you do so you will notice an increase in heat and energy. This same principle applies to the matter on the accretion disk in that energy associated with motion (kinetic energy) is transferred to heat.

Relativistic Jets

An amazing feature of the accretion disk is that strong fields, called electric and magnetic fields, are produced by the energetic particles involved in the accretion process. A byproduct of these fields is that vibrant jets of particles can begin to stream above and below the black hole. Black holes that produce these jets are considered active galactic nuclei. The jets signify if the black hole is active or not, while the term "galactic nuclei" accounts for the black hole residing at the center of the galaxy. In some cases, active galactic nuclei can outshine the light of the entire galaxy they reside in.[3]

Black Hole Merger

Once black holes are sufficiently close, strong interacting gravitational fields dominate and set the stage for a cataclysmic event, a black hole collision. In a process that is still not very well understood, the black holes, up to a billion solar masses each, undergo a spectacular merger into a single black hole. As this coalescence unfolds, extreme amounts of energy are

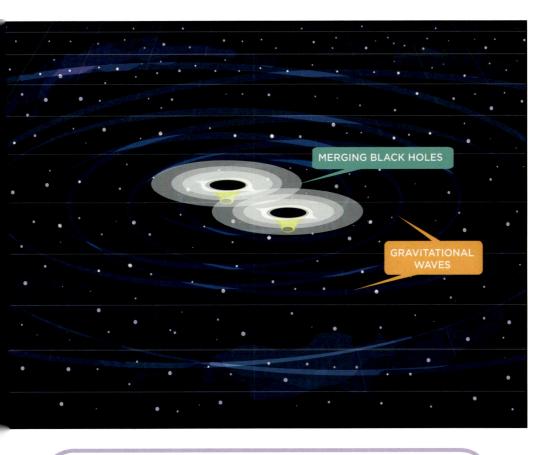

Two black holes collide. A byproduct of the merger is the creation of gravitational waves, or ripples in space, that can be detected from Earth.

BLACK HOLES EXPLAINED

produced in the process. In fact, the merger can be so powerful that gravitational waves can occur in the very fabric of space.[4] Visualize a collision of large objects in a body of water, such as two boats. Once the impact occurs, energy is then transferred in the form of ripples that move away from the initial point of contact. Similarly, merging black holes create waves, often detectable more than a billion light-years from the collision.[5]

Local Merger

The Milky Way may in fact experience a galactic merger. The closest galactic neighbor to the Milky Way is the Andromeda

This is the Andromeda galaxy, the Milky Way's closest neighbor. In approximately 4.5 billion years, the pair is expected to collide and form into a single black hole.

galaxy, a relatively close companion at only 2.5 million light-years away. The gravitational attraction between the two galaxies has initiated, and in roughly 4.5 billion years a collision is predicted to occur. The result of this event will be the merger of the supermassive black holes at the center of both galaxies. A unique set of gravitational waves will then ripple throughout space as two black holes become one.

Though black hole mergers have yet to be visually confirmed, instruments have been able to detect the signals from gravitational waves. Additionally, research teams are continuing to explore methods to study the behavior of mergers. Computer simulations have proven to be great resources to test theories on black hole merger frequency in the universe, as well as the additional effects on nearby matter from the merger.

The gravitational intensity of black holes, from stellar to supermassive, is in a class of its own. From the tremendous influence black holes have on matter, to their ability to inhibit light from escaping their cores, they have proven fascinating cosmic regions of space. Now consider what specifically happens as matter crosses the boundary of the center of a black hole. What if scientists slowed time down and analyzed this process? Are the laws of physics still valid here?

Chapter Five

The Event Horizon

The velocity necessary for a space-bound rocket to counter Earth's gravitational tug and depart the atmosphere is known as the escape velocity. It is the minimum speed required for an object to escape the gravitational influence of a larger body. For an object to counter the gravity of Earth, it would need a velocity of 6.8 miles (11 kilometers) per second. At this rate, one could travel from New York to California in approximately seven minutes!

Now, consider the sun is 332,946 times more massive than Earth and that the mass of a black hole can range from six to several billion solar masses. For supermassive black holes, this is equivalent to one hundred trillion Earth masses. How can a region this much more massive, and gravitationally stronger, than Earth affect matter and light close to it?

Black Hole Escape Velocity

The mass of a black hole is concentrated near its center. For matter and light within close proximity, this can lead to very interesting results. While Earth's escape velocity has been calculated at 6.8 miles per second, a black hole's core has an escape velocity that is actually greater than the speed of light. For reference, the speed of light is the velocity that light travels within the empty space of the universe; it is the fastest known speed matter or radiation can travel in the universe at 186,411 miles (300,000 km) per second.

If the speed of light is not fast enough to escape the gravity of a black hole's core, all other matter, which travels at speeds far less than this value, are destined to remain trapped in the black hole's gravitational field. Scientists classify the region where even light is trapped in a black hole as the Schwarzschild radius.

Schwarzschild Radius

In 1915 Einstein worked on formulating his framework for general relativity. In the process, he produced several fundamental equations that characterize how space and time curve as a function of the matter and energy in the universe. These equations are known as Einstein's field equations. The following year, German astronomer Karl Schwarzschild (1873–1916) obtained an exact solution for these equations.[1] His work led to the formation of the Schwarzschild radius, a region around the core of a black hole where matter and light cannot escape.

The boundary of a Schwarzschild radius marks the initiation of what is known as the event horizon. Matter and light that travel beyond this region are bound to a one-way trip, with

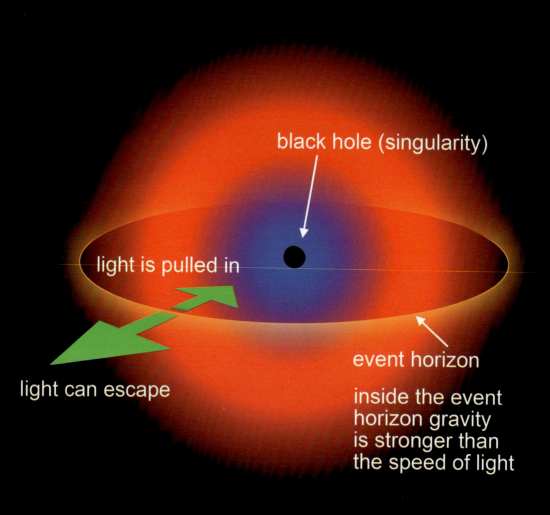

An artist's rendition of a black hole's event horizon is shown. Any closer to a black hole from this distance, and gravitational forces are so strong that nothing can escape, not even light.

no way out. Specifically, in-falling particles and radiation are unable to reenter the universe due to the extremely high escape velocity required.

Event Horizon

Astronomers face substantial challenges in understanding the dynamics of what occurs beyond the event horizon. In particular, observations are not possible in any wavelength because light and energy are not measurable once they pass into this region. Furthermore, theoretical computer simulations incorporate highly educated assumptions but are ultimately based on predictions rather than what can be observed beyond the event horizon. Comprehending this area becomes even more difficult because the laws of physics that attempt to understand the cosmos are not applicable here. Physicist Kip Thorne describes the event horizon as "the point where all laws of physics break down."[2]

KIP THORNE

Additionally, scientists consider the region beyond the event horizon not as a place in space or time. Rather, it is possible that matter that enters this region is destroyed and disappears from the universe.[3] As a result, an infinitely dense region is created that may tear through the very fabric of space. This region is termed the "singularity."

Non-Rotating Black Hole

Black holes can also be classified by whether or not they rotate. Non-rotating black holes are known as Schwarzschild black holes and represent the simplest kind of black holes, which have mass but no rotation. They are characterized by the Schwarzschild radius, which can also be considered the radius of the black hole. It is at this region that the event horizon is marked.

Rotating Black Hole

In 1963 New Zealand mathematician Roy Kerr (1934–) proposed an alternate type of black hole. Kerr provided mathematical justification for the Kerr black hole, a rotating black hole.[4] These black holes are in fact the most common in nature, and their rotation is caused by the rotation of stars that form them. Specifically, when the rotating star collapses, the core continues to rotate and this motion, known as angular momentum, is carried over to the black hole.

Once a star collapses and forms a Kerr black hole, the core becomes the singularity of the newly formed black hole. The boundary where the singularity begins marks the event horizon, where the gravitational field becomes infinitely dense. Additionally, around the event horizon there is a region known

THE EVENT HORIZON

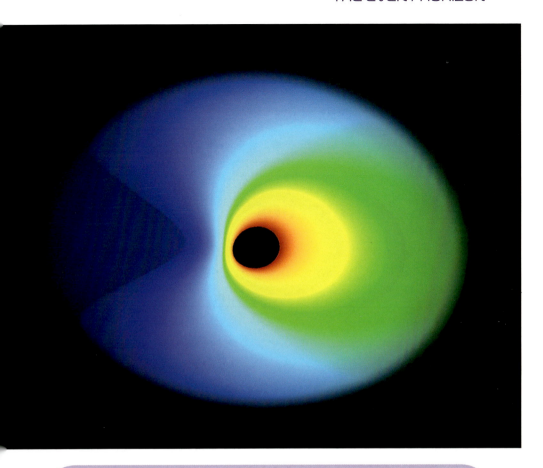

A computer model is shown that depicts a rotating black hole. Red indicates matter moving away from an observer (red shifted), and blue represents matter moving toward an observer (blue shifted). Near the center, matter rapidly falls in toward the core of the black hole and as a result is depicted as red. The center is black, as no light can escape the core of a black hole.

as the ergosphere, an egg-shaped region of distorted space caused by the spinning of the black hole, which "drags" the space around it. Finally, a unique feature of a Kerr black hole is termed the static limit, a boundary between the ergosphere and normal space.

Unlike a Schwarzschild black hole, Kerr black holes can eject objects that pass into the ergosphere. This is possible if an object can gain enough energy from the rotation of the black hole to be flung out. Similar to a Schwarzschild black hole, though, once matter crosses the event horizon it also cannot escape.

Black Hole Properties

Though black holes, rotating and non-rotating, cannot be observed directly, researchers can still infer many properties about them. Specifically, the mass and rotation speed for Kerr black holes can be measured by studying the movement of matter around the black hole. For example, if the mass of a star is known and is orbiting around a black hole, the velocity that it rotates will directly correspond to the mass and gravitational pull of the black hole.

Spaghettification

As particles fall into the event horizon of a black hole, whether the black hole is rotating or not, their physical structure undergoes radical changes. The process that unfolds is referred to as "spaghettification." As the name suggests, matter is vertically stretched and experiences horizontal compression into thin long shapes, like spaghetti! Regardless of the strength of the matter, the process of spaghettification can overcome it and force the matter to stretch. Astrophysicist Stephen Hawking described this process with reference to an astronaut approaching the core of a black hole head first. As the astronaut nears, the process of spaghettification would stretch the astronaut from head to toe. This is due to the gravitational force being much stronger at

THE EVENT HORIZON

Molecules are stripped apart as they fall into a black hole in a process known as spaghettification, where particles are stretched apart due to strong gravitational forces.

one end opposed to the other when approaching a black hole.[5] The difference in gravitational force is described as a gravitational gradient.

If matter and light can never escape the event horizon of a black hole, where does this matter go? Could matter passing through a black hole end up somewhere else in the universe, or another universe entirely?

45

Chapter Six

A Cosmic Worm

Matter and radiation that funnel into a black hole are likely destined to remain trapped within its gravitational field. Effectively, they become isolated from space once past the event horizon. For matter that experiences this immense gravitational tug, it is stretched apart and broken down into subatomic particles that journey into the black hole's singularity. However, at this point, where density becomes infinite, the laws of physics break down. As a result, exotic regions of space have been proposed to explain what occurs beyond the singularity.

Wormholes

In 1935 Albert Einstein and physicist Nathan Rosen (1909–1995) continued work on the theory of general relativity to better comprehend black holes. After several attempts to solve the equations of relativity, a unique type of object in the universe was theorized to exist based on the calculations. Specifically, the equations led to the concept of Einstein-Rosen bridges, or wormholes.[1] The equations demonstrated that a wormhole could serve as a bridge in space.[2] Though frequently a topic of science

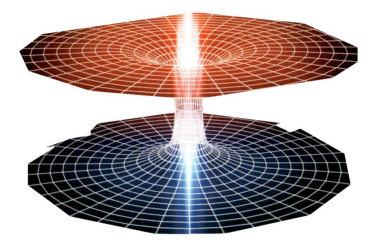

Theoretically, wormholes can serve as bridges between regions in space and are believed to arise from matter falling through the center of a black hole.

fiction, these theoretical regions are believed to exist throughout space and can serve as shortcuts that cut across the universe. These regions are predicted to contain two spheroidal mouths, with a throat-like bridge connecting the two.

Imagine lightly bending a sheet of paper so that half of the sheet is curved below the other half, being sure not to form a crease. If one wants to travel to a location on the lower half, the traditional route to take would be to travel on the outer surface of the sheet and move along the curvature of the paper. Drawing a line from a point on the upper half around to a point directly

BLACK HOLES EXPLAINED

below on the lower half will provide a good sense of the distance required. In space, one would also travel along a surface, the fabric of space itself, to journey to a distant point.

However, the concept of a wormhole eliminates the need to journey in such a lengthy path; rather, a bridge can exist that enables travel directly through the paper. Travel between a point on the top half of the sheet of paper to a point below on the lower half can then be made without needing to travel across the surface of the paper; one would just go straight through. Consider pushing a sharpened pencil straight through the sheet from a point on the upper half to a point directly under on the lower half. In space, this bridge would be equivalent to a wormhole.

Furthermore, scientists believe that if wormholes do exist and are stable, information could be passed through them. This would indicate that wormholes could be a bridge not only between locations in the universe, but also between different universes.

White Hole

There is yet another fascinating region of space linked to black holes. In particular, Sergey Solodukhin of International University Bremen in Germany strongly supports the existence of regions in the universe that may be reverse black holes. He suggests that as matter passes through a black hole, it may eventually be ejected out of what is termed a white hole, based on theoretical mathematical concepts.[3] Consider that matter and radiation are pulled rapidly into a black hole, shrinking and being pulled apart in the process. However, a point is reached when they can no longer be stretched and reduced in size further. At this point, a hypothetical white hole may exist at the end of a worm hole, where matter and energy can pass through the other side of the black hole.[4]

Matter passing through the center of a black hole is theorized to pass through a white hole (depicted here) formed at the other end.

Detection Limitations

Despite theoretical claims, wormholes and white holes have not yet been detected. This is so because these regions lie near or within the singularity, where light cannot escape and the laws of physics break down. As a result, mathematical computations and computer simulations remain the best sources for analyzing these proposed regions.

Future Research

In 2006, astronomers believed they may have found evidence for the existence of a white hole. Specifically, they measured high-energy gamma bursts that were detected with no obvious source, such as a supernova. Astronomers suggested this may have been a white hole observation. However, this remains debated and follow-up work is required.[5]

WHITE HOLE DETECTION

Gamma ray bursts are the most energetic explosions in the universe. In late May 2011, a report was generated that a known gamma ray burst, GRB 060614, may have been a white hole.[6]

Provided white holes are the theoretical opposite of black holes, they would radiate light and potentially gamma rays. GRB 060614

A COSMIC WORM

was detected on June 14, 2006, but it did not have typical characteristics of gamma ray bursts. Specifically, gamma ray bursts often occur in regions of low star formation or are associated with a supernova. GRB 06014 has neither of those properties and is believed to potentially be a radiating white hole.

Gamma ray bursts create high-energy radiation that journeys throughout the universe. Scientists believe these events could be tied to white holes.

BLACK HOLES EXPLAINED

For comparison, consider the progress achieved in analyzing black holes. These regions had yet to be detected until the late twentieth century. However, significant strides have been made that provide important details on their nature. For example, it is believed that every galaxy in the universe contains at least one supermassive black hole and that matter near black holes can be studied in X-ray. Thus, while very little is currently understood about wormholes and white holes, astronomers are hopeful more will be understood as observational tools improve.

Black holes are immense cannibalizing cosmic entities that only seem to grow in size. However, there may also exist an entirely different type of black hole, a miniature black hole. What processes could form these small regions? Could scientists replicate one?

Chapter Seven

Miniature Black Holes

In 1971 Stephen Hawking proposed the theory of micro black holes, a hypothetical class of small-scale black holes that exist within the universe.[1]

Matter during the early universe, when it was very hot and not yet solidified (soupy), was constantly mashed together and flung apart. Occasionally, though, some regions stuck together and got very dense. This caused some matter to collapse on itself and form miniature lumps. Hawking suggests that many of these lumps formed into micro black holes, some less than the size of an atom.[2]

Temperature Characteristics

The gravitational strength of a black hole increases as it gets smaller. Additionally, as a black hole gets smaller, its temperature increases.

Thus, massive black holes have weaker gravitational fields than smaller ones. This weaker gravitational field causes matter to orbit slower around the black hole, which results in a lower amount of energy radiated away, and thus lower temperatures. For example, the most massive black holes in the universe have temperatures near absolute zero, the coldest temperature measurable in the universe.

Comparatively, micro black holes can be very hot due to their strong gravitational fields, where matter is forced to rotate faster about the event horizon and heat up.[3] For mini black holes near one-thousandth the mass of the moon, they can have a temperature near 1,700 kelvins (2600° F or 1427° C), more than five times the surface temperature of Earth!

For reference, Hawking mentioned "a mountain-sized black hole would give off X-rays and gamma-rays at a rate of about 10 million megawatts, enough to power the world's electricity supply."[4] Hawking was alluding to the extreme temperatures present in very small black holes due to the high energy they emit.

Gravitational Strength

Spaghettification is the fate of matter approaching the singularity of a black whole. A small black hole, roughly the size of an average human, will exert a significantly larger force than a large black hole of the same mass. For these classes of black holes, the spaghettification process would actually occur outside of the event horizon, whereas this process would occur very near to the event horizon for a massive black hole.[5] This is so because gravitational strength increases as black hole size is reduced.

TEMPERATURE IN THE UNIVERSE

Absolute zero is the coldest temperature measurable in the universe. It corresponds to zero kelvin, where kelvins are common units of temperature measurement in astronomy. One kelvin equals -457.87° F or -272.15° C.

(continued on the next page)

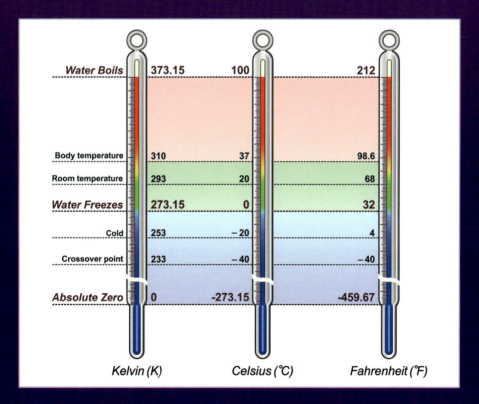

This chart shows the conversion of Kelvin to degrees Celsius and Fahrenheit.

BLACK HOLES EXPLAINED

(continued from the previous page)

Earth's surface is approximately 300 kelvins, which is about 80.33°F or 26.85°C.

Comparatively, the average temperature of the universe today is 2.73 kelvins (-454.76° F or 270.42° C). This temperature is based on measurements of cosmic background radiation, which is radiation left over from the early stages of the universe. This radiation is noticeable as a faint glow if one were to use a radio telescope pointed at the space in between stars and galaxies.

Dark Matter

Dark matter is a hypothetical form of matter that exists in the universe. It has been named as such because similar to black holes, it cannot be detected directly. Dark matter is responsible for a number of observations in the universe that currently cannot be accounted for otherwise. Specifically, scientists observe matter, dust, and stars being attracted to regions in space that cannot be seen, regions assumed to be comprised of dark matter. Furthermore, light emitted from distant objects in the universe, such as galaxies, experience a slight bending of their path as they journey toward Earth and are observed; this bending of light is called gravitational lensing and is considered to be partially attributed to the gravitational pull of dark matter in the universe. Additional events in the universe that are associated with dark matter include the structure of large-scale objects and the formation of galaxies.

MINIATURE BLACK HOLES

The cluster of galaxies (yellow) in the center is about five billion light years away. The blue arcs are distant galaxies magnified and distorted by gravitational lensing.

In fact, dark matter is so substantial that it is believed to make up nearly one-fourth of the mass in the universe.[6]

Provided the abundance of dark matter in the universe, detectors on both Earth and in space have been used by scientists

BLACK HOLES EXPLAINED

for decades to discover the origins of the matter; however, no definitive results have been achieved.

A new theory, formulated by astrophysicists Vyacheslav Dokuchaev and Yury Eroshenko at the Institute for Nuclear Research and the Russian Academy of Sciences in Moscow, suggests that dark matter could actually stem from microscopic black holes.[7] Similar to dark matter, black holes do not emit light and are not directly detectable by telescopes. In particular, micro black holes close in mass to an asteroid and smaller than an atom would be dark, extremely dense, and massive, exactly the criteria needed for classification as a dark matter candidate.

However, other astronomers have doubts regarding the theory that micro black holes could be dark matter candidates. For example, Avi Leob, an astrophysicist at Harvard University, mentions that accretion, or the flow of matter into a black hole, should be associated with black holes. Because this feature is not present in dark matter as far as scientists can infer, micro black holes may be invalidated as dark matter candidates.[8] Ultimately, much uncertainty still remains about dark matter.

Search for Signs

The strong gravitational pull proposed to exist for micro black holes, compared to larger black holes, would lead to higher temperatures near its event horizon. As a result, it should theoretically be easier to detect these objects in the universe compared to their larger companions. However, observations of these objects have yet to occur. For reference, NASA scientists were able to detect the smallest black hole to date, weighing 3.8 times the mass of the sun; however, this black hole is still not small or light enough to be considered a micro black hole.

Scientists do believe that such an object could be discovered with improving observational equipment, though. In particular, mass calculations have been relied upon for other classes of black holes and should be transferrable. For example, one of the lowest mass black holes observed to date was detected using X-ray detection in 2001 with the Rossi X-Ray Timing Explorer satellite. To weigh the black hole, astronomers used the relationship between the size of the black hole and the gas that swirls into the black hole's disk. As the gas condenses near the black hole, it heats up and radiates X-rays. The intensity of the X-rays varies over time and provides a frequency signal. The signal is directly related to the mass of the black hole; thus, astronomers can determine how heavy the black hole is and use this method for other black holes, specifically micro black holes.[9]

In addition, researchers have considered the possibility of creating miniature black holes on Earth. To do so they have relied upon Einstein's special theory of relativity, proposed in 1905, which theorized that anything having a mass has an equivalent amount of energy and vice versa.[10] Specifically, it may be possible to use the Large Hadron Collider (LHC), a large-scale physics experiment in Geneva, Switzerland, to rapidly accelerate particles much smaller than an atom at each other to create a high-speed collision.[11] As these particles collide, a vast amount of energy is created. Consequently, a vast amount of mass is formed. Hypothetically, a collision could then produce enough mass in a small enough space to form a black hole.

While a black hole could theoretically be created at the LHC, estimates predict it would evaporate almost immediately due to its small size. Additionally, no black holes have yet been formed at the LHC, though scientists support the notion that the possibility still exists.

BLACK HOLES EXPLAINED

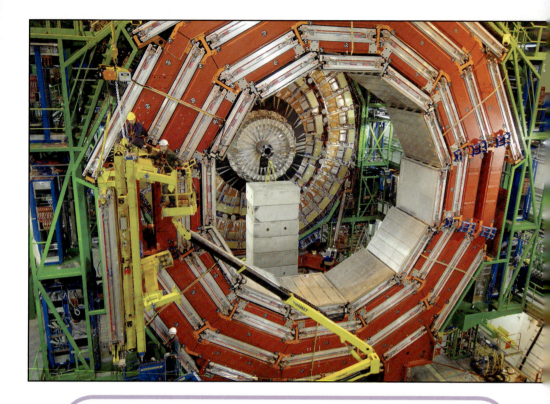

> This is a component of the Large Hadron Collider, a machine that rapidly accelerates particles at high speeds toward each other, creating energetic collisions that may have the potential to form micro black holes.

Black holes can be massive enough to influence the fundamental structure and behavior of matter within their host galaxy. They may also exist as micro-scale objects, less than the size of an atom. For both types of extremes, is it possible for them to experience death? If so, what processes are involved as they depart the universe?

Chapter Eight

A Black Hole's Fate

Black holes feed on matter within close proximity and experience continuous growth as a result. However, over a long enough time, will they cease to exist? Additionally, a number of black hole paradoxes exist that seem to violate the laws of physics. How can astronomers resolve them?

Hawking Radiation

Stephen Hawking considered the region near the event horizon of a black hole in great detail for small black holes. In 1974 he postulated what is now termed "Hawking radiation."[1] Hawking proposed the idea that for every particle falling into an event horizon, there exists what is known as an antiparticle.

Imagine a single electron, with a negative charge, traveling into the event horizon of a black hole. Hawking believed that a particle intimately connected to this electron with the same

BLACK HOLES EXPLAINED

Hawking radiation (blue) escapes a black hole. It is theorized that for every particle that falls into a black hole, a small amount of radiation is emitted.

mass but opposite charge would also exist. This particle would be called a positron, for its positive charge. The theory of Hawking radiation indicates that for an electron, or any particle, that crosses into the event horizon of a moderately sized black hole, an antiparticle, such as a positron, is emitted. Thus, the black hole is capable of producing its own radiation, powered by the gravitational pull of the core.

STEPHEN HAWKING

Stephen Hawking was a renowned theoretical physicist and cosmologist born on January 8, 1942, in Oxford, England. He passed away in March of 2018.

In 1974, Hawking received much acclaim for his theory that

(continued on the next page)

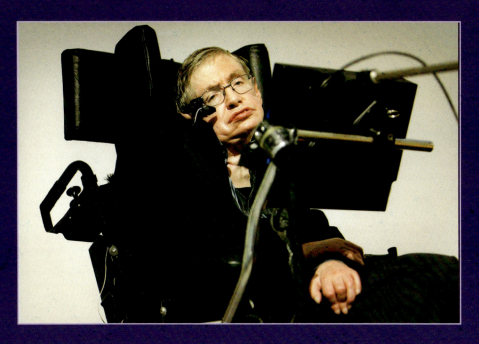

Astrophysicist Stephen Hawking delivers a speech in 2007. Hawking was responsible for pivotal contributions to the field, including the theory of Hawking radiation and gravitational singularities.

(continued from the previous page)

radiation could escape the gravitational force of a collapsed star that became a black hole. This radiation was eventually termed Hawking radiation.

Hawking also proposed the theory of the gravitational singularity in 1968, a region of infinite density where the laws of physics break down. In fact, Hawking supported the notion that the universe may have started as a singularity.

He also postulated that the event horizon of a black hole, where not even light can escape, can never get smaller.

Black Hole Death

Black holes cannibalize matter in their proximity, and it could be assumed that they experience infinite growth. However, scientists propose that all black holes eventually evaporate over time.[2] This is due to Hawking radiation. As matter is stretched, heated, and pulled closer toward the gravitational tug of the core, the matter heats up and energy is radiated away. Over a long enough timescale, this results in mass of the black hole being lost. Eventually, the black hole can lose enough mass to evaporate. Calculations have shown, though, that it would take far longer for massive black holes to evaporate than the current age of the universe![3]

In comparison, micro black holes experience a different fate. Calculations show that the smaller the size of a black hole, the faster the evaporation rate. For a micro black hole, this results in an explosion of particles almost immediately. Particularly, the approximate limit for a black hole to evaporate is 0.02 milligrams, roughly the mass of a flea egg.[4] In the process of evaporating down to this mass, the black hole becomes hotter and hotter as it emits radiating energy. Once the minimum mass threshold is met and the particle begins to evaporate from the universe, the object can no longer be described as a traditional black hole, and the laws of physics and Hawking's calculations can no longer be used to predict the state of the object.

The Information Paradox

For non-rotating and rotating black holes, a number of mysteries continue to puzzle astronomers. The primary paradox regarding black holes is termed as the "information paradox."

The information paradox considers that the matter, and information, passing beyond the event horizon of a black hole are lost from the universe. However, as a black hole evaporates, it emits Hawking radiation. Through this process, mass enters the event horizon in a pure state and an antiparticle returns to the universe. Though the antiparticle is believed to return in what is called a mixed form, a form that offers no information about the particle that produced the antiparticle.[5] The fact that a black hole can take matter in a pure state and convert it to a mixed state violates what is known as quantum unitarity. This is a restriction in physics that ensures consistency when dealing with systems of atoms and subatomic particles and assures information is not lost in the universe.

To resolve this paradox, scientists have developed the "firewall proposal." In this proposal, the event horizon would actually be replaced by a firewall, a boundary where the event horizon would emit outgoing streams of radiation. For an observer falling into a black hole, they would be destroyed as they approach this region, and the region beyond the firewall would be inaccessible to the outside universe. This would assure information would not be lost and that information carried in by the observer in a pure state is absorbed at the firewall and returned to the universe in a pure state when radiated back. The information paradox would thus be avoided and quantum unitarity maintained.

Scientific Understanding

Black holes do eventually evaporate as they lose mass through Hawking radiation. However, while they are active, their influence on matter, radiation, and galactic evolution can reveal many astronomical phenomena that occur throughout the universe. For example, measurements of gravitational waves made by LIGO have equipped scientists with knowledge of how the fabric of space responds to merging black holes; analyzing the motion of stars, dust, and other matter near the cores of black holes has shed light on accretion disks that funnel particles onto black hole cores and produce jets of radiation; and observations of the Milky Way's supermassive black hole, Sagittarius A*, have offered initial evidence that a supermassive black hole exists at the center of the galaxy.

In addition, micro black holes may possibly reveal the nature of dark matter, an astronomical mystery that has puzzled scientists for decades.

Much has been learned about black holes to date; however, there are many milestones to be achieved as space agencies such as NASA and the European Space Agency (ESA) focus on learning more about these entities. In addition, universities across the globe, such as the California Institute of Technology and the University of Cambridge, have also directed their attention toward black hole astronomy and continue to refine their instruments to study black holes. Several missions devoted to analyzing black holes are pending and more continue to be proposed with the hope that the ability to detect black holes directly may eventually be realized.

CHAPTER NOTES

Introduction

1. Dan Falk, "Physicists Spot Einstein's Gravitational Waves for the First Time," Mental Floss, February 11, 2016, http://mentalfloss.com/article/75303/physicists-spot-einsteins-gravitational-waves-first-time.

2. Ashley Morrow, ed., "NSF's LIGO Has Detected Gravitational Waves," NASA, updated August 4, 2017, https://www.nasa.gov/feature/goddard/2016/nsf-s-ligo-has-detected-gravitational-waves.

3. "Gravitational Waves Detected 100 Years After Einstein's Prediction," LIGO Caltech, https://www.ligo.caltech.edu/news/ligo20160211.

4. Dennis Overbye, "Third Gravitational Wave Detection from Black-Hole Merger 3 Billion Light Years Away," *New York Time*s, June 1, 2017, https://www.nytimes.com/2017/06/01/science/black-holes-collision-ligo-gravitational-waves.html?mcubz=1.

5. Elizabeth Howell, "Monster Black Hole Is Biggest Ever Found," Space.com, November 28, 2012, https://www.space.com/18668-biggest-black-hole-discovery.html.

6. "Black Holes," NASA, accessed January 11, 2018, https://science.nasa.gov/astrophysics/focus-areas/black-holes.

7. Fraser Cain, "How Much of the Universe Is Black Holes?" Universe Today, updated March 2, 2017, https://www.universetoday.com/112500/how-much-of-the-universe-is-black-holes/.

8. Karen Northon, ed., "NASA Selects Mission to Study Black Holes, Cosmic X-ray Mysteries," NASA, updated August 4, 2017, https://www.nasa.gov/press-release/nasa-selects-mission-to-study-black-holes-cosmic-x-ray-mysteries.

CHAPTER NOTES

Chapter One
The Birth of a Giant

1. Karl Hille, "Hubble Reveals Observable Universe Contains 10 Times More Galaxies Than Previously Thought," NASA, updated August 4, 2017, https://www.nasa.gov/feature/goddard/2016/hubble-reveals-observable-universe-contains-10-times-more-galaxies-than-previously-thought.
2. Tom Henderson, "Newton's Law of Universal Gravitation," Physics Classroom, http://www.physicsclassroom.com/class/circles/Lesson-3/Newton-s-Law-of-Universal-Gravitation.
3. "A New Kind of Black Hole," NASA, https://www.nasa.gov/vision/universe/starsgalaxies/Black_Hole.html.
4. Mike Wall, "It's Confirmed! Black Holes Do Come in Medium Sizes," Space.com, August 18, 2014, https://www.space.com/26857-medium-size-black-hole-discovery-m82.html.
5. Ibid.

Chapter Two
A Galactic Heart

1. Nola Taylor Redd, "Milky Way Galaxy: Facts About Our Galactic Home," Space.com, June 12, 2017, https://www.space.com/19915-milky-way-galaxy.html.
2. Ronald J. Buta, "Galaxy Types: Stage, Family, and Variety," NASA/IPAC Extragalactic Database, February 2, 2011, https://ned.ipac.caltech.edu/level5/Sept11/Buta/Buta5.html.
3. Fraser Cain, "Why Are There Black Holes in the Middle of Galaxies," Universe Today, updated December 24, 2015, https://www.universetoday.com/13732/why-are-there-black-holes-in-the-middle-of-galaxies/.

BLACK HOLES EXPLAINED

4. "General Relativity," Einstein Online, accessed January 11, 2018, http://www.einstein-online.info/elementary/generalRT/index.html/index.html@searchterm=None.html.

5. Clara Moskowitz, "Massive Black Hole Bends Light to Magnify Distant Galaxy," Space.com, July 27, 2010, https://www.space.com/8830-massive-black-hole-bends-light-magnify-distant-galaxy.html.

6. "Live from Keck Observatory: The Supermassive Black Hole," W. M. Keck Observatory, July 7, 2014, http://www.keckobservatory.org/recent/entry/live_from_keck_observatory_the_supermassive_black_hole.

Chapter Three
Cosmic Exploration

1. Nola Taylor Redd, "Einstein's Theory of General Relativity," Space.com, November 7, 2017, https://www.space.com/17661-theory-general-relativity.html.

2. "Cygnus X-1," Constellation Guide, June 19, 2014, http://www.constellation-guide.com/cygnus-x-1/.

3. "Discovering the Electromagnetic Spectrum," NASA, September 2013, https://imagine.gsfc.nasa.gov/science/toolbox/history_multiwavelength1.html.

4. "Swift Overview," NASA, updated August 3, 2017, https://www.nasa.gov/mission_pages/swift/overview/index.html.

5. Dr. David Whitehouse, "Blast Hints at Black Hole Birth," BBC News, May 11, 2005, http://news.bbc.co.uk/2/hi/science/nature/4537905.stm.

6. "About Chandra," Chandra X-Ray Observatory, accessed November 22, 2017, http://chandra.harvard.edu/about/.

CHAPTER NOTES

7. Susanna Kohler, "LIGO Discovers the Merger of Two Black Holes," AAS NOVA, February 11, 2016, http://aasnova.org/2016/02/11/ligo-discovers-the-merger-of-two-black-holes/.

Chapter Four
Merging Companions

1. "What Is the Average Distance Between Galaxies?" Quora. com, accessed November 22, 2017, https://www.quora.com/What-is-the-average-distance-between-galaxies.
2. Kate Kershner, "What's an Accretion Disk?" Howstuffworks. com, accessed November 22, 2017, http://science. howstuffworks.com/accretion-disk.htm.
3. "Relativistic Jets," NuSTAR, accessed November 22, 2017, https://www.nustar.caltech.edu/page/relativistic_jets.
4. "What Happens When Black Holes Collide?" HubbleSite, accessed November 22, 2017, http://hubblesite.org/explore_astronomy/black_holes/encyc_mod3_q6.html.
5. Fraser Cain, "What Happens When Black Holes Collide," Universe Today, updated October 5, 2017, https://www.universetoday.com/131212/happens-black-holes-collide/.

Chapter Five
The Event Horizon

1. Luke Mastin, "Karl Schwarzschild (1873–1916)," Physics of the Universe, 2009, http://www.physicsoftheuniverse.com/scientists_schwarzschild.html.

71

BLACK HOLES EXPLAINED

2. Luke Mastin, "Singularities," Physics of the Universe, 2009, http://www.physicsoftheuniverse.com/topics_blackholes_singularities.html.

3. "How Can a Singularity Have Infinite Density?" Quora.com, accessed November 22, 2017, https://www.quora.com/How-can-a-singularity-have-infinite-density.

4. Craig Freudenrich, "How Black Holes Work," Howstuffworks.com, accessed November 22, 2017, http://science.howstuffworks.com/dictionary/astronomy-terms/black-hole2.htm.

5. William Harris, "What If You Fell into a Black Hole?" Howstuffworks.com, accessed November 22, 2017, https://science.howstuffworks.com/science-vs-myth/what-if/what-if-fell-into-black-hole2.htm.

Chapter Six
A Cosmic Worm

1. Nola Taylor Redd, "What Is a Wormhole?" Space.com, October 20, 2017, https://www.space.com/20881-wormholes.html.

2. Ibid.

3. Mitchell C. Begelman, "Evidence for Black Holes," *Science* 300, no. 5627 (2003): pp. 1898–1903, jstor.org/stable/3834516.

4. Fraser Cain, "What Are White Holes?" Phys.org, October 9, 2015, https://phys.org/news/2015-10-white-holes.html.

5. Deborah Byrd, "Do White Holes Exist?" EarthSky, May 27, 2011, http://earthsky.org/space/have-we-seen-a-white-hole.

6. Ibid.

CHAPTER NOTES

Chapter Seven
Miniature Black Holes

1. Stephen Hawking, "Gravitationally Collapsed Objects of Very Low Mass," *Monthly Notices of the Royal Astronomical Society* 152, no. 1, April 1, 1971: pp. 75–78, https://doi.org/10.1093/mnras/152.1.75.

2. Philip Ball, "These Are the Discoveries That Made Stephen Hawking Famous," BBC.com, January 7, 2016, http://www.bbc.com/earth/story/20160107-these-are-the-discoveries-that-made-stephen-hawking-famous.

3. Sabine Hossenfelder, "Micro Black Holes," *Backreaction,* September 22, 2006, http://backreaction.blogspot.com/2006/09/micro-black-holes.html.

4. Stephen Hawking, "Into a Black Hole," Stephen Hawking Official Website, 2008, http://www.hawking.org.uk/into-a-black-hole.html.

5. Esther Inglis-Arkell, "Here's Why Small Black Holes Are More Dangerous Than Big Ones," io9.gizmodo.com, January 27, 2015, https://io9.gizmodo.com/heres-why-small-black-holes-are-more-dangerous-than-big-1681979641.

6. "Planck Mission Brings Universe into Sharp Focus," NASA, updated May 7, 2014,https://www.nasa.gov/mission_pages/planck/news/planck20130321.html.

7. Katia Moskvitch, "Could Tiny Black Hole Atoms Be Elusive Dark Matter?" Space.com, April 30, 2014, https://www.space.com/25691-dark-matter-black-hole-atoms.html.

8. Ibid.

BLACK HOLES EXPLAINED

9. Andrea Thompson, "Smallest Black Hole Found," Space .com, April 1, 2008, https://www.space.com/5191-smallest -black-hole.html.

10. Matt Strassler, "How Did Einstein Do It?," Of Particular Significance, accessed November 28, 2017, https:// profmattstrassler.com/articles-and-posts/particle-physics- basics/mass-energy-matter-etc/mass-and-energy/ how-did-einstein-do-it/.

11. Charles Q. Choi, "Mini Black Holes Easier to Make Than Thought," LiveScience, March 12, 2013, https://www. livescience.com/27811-creating-mini-black-holes.html.

Chapter Eight
A Black Hole's Fate

1. "All About Black Holes," Tumbleweed Observatory's Astronomy Hints, accessed November 28, 2017, http://www. astronomyhints.com/blackholes.html.

2. Fraser Cain, "How Do Black Holes Evaporate," Universe Today, updated February 27, 2017, https://www.universetoday. com/119794/how-do-black-holes-evaporate/.

3. "What Would the Death of a Black Hole Look Like?" *Slate,* November 12, 2013, http://www.slate.com/blogs/ quora/2013/11/12/what_would_the_death_of_a_black_hole_ look_like.html.

4. Eben Alexander and Karen Newell, *Living in a Mindful Universe: A Neurosurgeon's Journey into the Heart of Consciousness* (Harlan, IA: Rodale Books, 2017), p. 259.

5. Pankaj S. Joshi and Ramesh Narayan, "Black Hole Paradoxes," *Journal of Physics* 759 (2016), http://iopscience.iop.org/ article/10.1088/1742-6596/759/1/012060/pdf.

GLOSSARY

accretion The process of particles sticking together to form larger bodies; for example, planetesimals accreted to form planets.

angular momentum The quantity of rotation of a body, which is the product of its moment of inertia and angular velocity.

atom The basic unit of a chemical element.

dark matter A term used to describe matter in the universe that cannot be seen but can be detected by its gravitational effect on other bodies.

density The amount of matter contained within a given volume.

ergosphere The region located outside a rotating black hole's outer event horizon.

escape velocity The speed required for an object to escape the gravitational pull of a planet or other body.

event horizon The invisible boundary around a black hole past which nothing can escape the gravitational pull, not even light.

fusion A process where nuclei collide so fast they stick together and emit a great deal of energy.

galactic nucleus A tight concentration of stars and gas found at the innermost regions of a galaxy.

galaxy A large system of about one hundred billion stars.

gravitational lensing A concentration of matter, such as a galaxy or cluster of galaxies, that bends light rays from a background object.

gravitational wave A ripple in the curvature of space-time that travels as a wave at the speed of light, generated in certain gravitational interactions that travel outward from their source.

BLACK HOLES EXPLAINED

Hawking radiation Electromagnetic radiation that, according to theory, should be emitted by a black hole.

light-year The distance light travels in a year, at the rate of 186,000 miles (300,000 kilometers) per second.

matter Anything that contains mass.

molecule A group of atoms bonded together.

radiation Energy emitted in the form of waves of particles; photons.

relativistic jets Outflow of ionized matter.

singularity The center of a black hole, where the curvature of space-time is maximal.

space-time The concept of time and three-dimensional space regarded as fused in a four-dimensional continuum.

spectrum Electromagnetic radiation arranged in order of wavelength.

star A giant ball of hot gas that creates and emits its own radiation through nuclear fusion.

supernova The death explosion of a massive star.

wavelength The distance from crest to crest or trough to trough of an electromagnetic wave.

X-ray Electromagnetic radiation of a very short wavelength and very high energy.

FURTHER READING

Books

Bartusiak, Marcia. *Black Hole: How an Idea Abandoned by Newtonians, Hated by Einstein, and Gambled On by Hawking Became Loved*. New Haven, CT: Yale University Press, 2015.

Binney, James. *Astrophysics: A Very Short Introduction*. Oxford, UK: Oxford University Press, 2016.

Blundell, Katherine. *Black Holes: A Very Short Introduction*. Oxford, UK: Oxford University Press, 2015.

deGrasse Tyson, Neil, and Shelby Alinsky, ed. *StarTalk*. Washington, DC: National Geographic Children's Books, 2018.

DK. *Space!* New York, NY: DK Publishing, 2015.

Latta, Sara. *Black Holes: The Weird Science of the Most Mysterious Objects in the Universe*. Minneapolis, MN: Twenty-First Century Books, 2017.

Tolish, Alexander. *Gravity Explained.* New York, NY: Enslow Publishing, 2019.

BLACK HOLES EXPLAINED

Websites

NASA Science

science.nasa.gov/astrophysics/focus-areas/black-holes

Provides an overview of black holes, as well as an updated list of recent black hole news and discoveries.

National Geographic

www.nationalgeographic.com/science/space/universeblack-holes/

Learn more about black hole formation and its life cycle.

Space.com

www.space.com/15421-black-holes-facts-formation-discovery-sdcmp.html

Offers facts, theories, and a review of black holes.

INDEX

A

absolute zero, 54–55
ancient astronomy, 10, 12

B

black holes
  birth of, 9, 11–17
  as centers of galaxies, 8–9,
    18–20, 32–34
  cores of, 9, 19, 26, 34,
    39–45, 62, 64–66
  death of, 64–66
  gravitational pull of, 7–8,
    13–17, 19–23, 26, 39,
    43–45, 53–54, 64
  mergers of, 6, 17, 28, 31–37
  microscopic-sized, 53–60
  rotating vs. non-rotating, 42–44
  study of, 24–30
  supermassive-sized, 15–17,
    18–20, 22–23, 27, 32, 37, 38

C

Chandra X-Ray Observatory, 27
Cygnus X-1, 24–25, 26–27

D

dark matter, 56–58, 66

E

Einstein, Albert, 6, 21, 23, 39,
    46, 59
elliptical galaxies, 20–21
ergosphere, 43–44
escape velocity, 38–39
evaporation, 64–66
event horizon, 39–45, 54,
    61–62, 65–66

G

galactic nuclei, 34
galaxies
  distance between, 31
  mergers of, 31–37
  number of, 11
  size of, 9
  types of, 20
gamma rays, 27, 50–51
general relativity, 21–23, 39, 46
gravitational lensing, 21–22,
    56–57
gravitational waves, 6, 27–29,
    35–37, 41
gravity, theories of, 13, 21–23

H

Hawking, Stephen, 44, 53–54,
    61–65

BLACK HOLES EXPLAINED

Hawking radiation, 61–66
Herschel, William, 25–26

I

information paradox, 65–66
intermediate-mass black
  holes, 15–17

K

Kerr, Roy, 42–44

L

Large Hadron Collider, 59–60
Laser Interferometer
  Gravitational-Wave
  Observatory (LIGO), 6,
  27–30, 41
lenticular galaxies, 20–21
light, 11, 14, 19, 22–23, 25–26,
  39–41, 56

M

Milky Way, 8–9, 18–20, 27,
  36–37
miniature black holes, 53–60,
  64–66

N

NASA, 9, 27, 29, 58
Newton, Isaac, 13
non-rotating black holes, 42

R

radiation, 56, 61–66
relativistic jets, 34
relativity, 21–23, 39, 46, 59
rotating black holes, 42–44

S

Sagittarius A*, 9, 18–20, 27
Schwarzschild radius, 39–41, 42
singularity, 42, 46, 50, 54, 64
spaghettification, 44–45, 54
special relativity, 59
spiral galaxies, 20–21, 32
stars
  black holes from, 9, 11–17
  number of, 10–11
stellar black holes, 9, 11–17

T

temperature, 19, 25, 53–56
Thorne, Kip, 6, 41

W

waves, gravitational, 6, 27–29,
  35–37, 41
white holes, 48–52
wormholes, 46–48, 50

X

X-ray emissions, 26–27, 59